ACHING MIRACLE

Other books by Elina Petrova:

Белая площадь - сборник стихов, АОЗТ Издательство
Донеччина, Донецк, 1998.
WHITE SQUARE - A BOOK OF POEMS, Donetchina Publishing
House, Donetsk, Ukraine, 1998.

Selected other European publications by Elina Petrova:

"Арион," Москва, 2001, 2 / №30.
"Arion," Moscow, 2001. [poetry]

"Новая Юность," Москва, 1999, 4 / №37.
"Novaya Yunost," Moscow, 1999. [poetry]

"Глагол," Москва, 1993.
"Glagol," Moscow, 1993. [winners, First International
Contest of Russian Poetry]

"Соты," Киев, 2005, №12; 2001, №4.
"Soti," Kiev, 2005, 12 and 2001, 4. [poetry]

"Дикое поле," Донецк, 2006, №10; 2005, №7; 2003, №3;
2002, №1.
"Wild Field," Donetsk, 2006, 10; 2005, 7; 2003, 3;
2002, 1. [reviews]

"Четыре сантиметра Луны," междунар. лит.-худ.
альманах - Донецк, 2011, №4; 2010, №3.
"Four Centimeters of the Moon," Donetsk, 2011, 4
and 2010, 3. [translations of American and British poetry]

Aching Miracle

Poems by
Elina Petrova

Printed in the United States of America.

Library of Congress Control Number: 2015941590

ISBN: 978-0-692-42162-8
(poetry non-fiction)

Petrova, Elina
Aching Miracle
First edition

Cover photography: The Omega/Swan Nebula (M17)
— image STScI-2003-13 [modified] from Hubble website:
hubblesite.org/newscenter/archive/releases/2003/13/image/a/

Editing, cover design, and book graphics by Glynn Monroe Irby.
- poetry text font: Constantia 11.5 pt
- title page font: Ashbury-Light

All references to specific bird species have been capitalized in accord with grammatical style advanced by the International Ornithological Congress (IOC).

Fairdale Press
9801 Westheimer, Suite 302
Houston, Texas 77042

3   5   7   9   10   8   6   4   2

Acknowledgments

Thanks to the editors of magazines, anthologies, and websites in which these and other poems first appeared —

Harbinger Asylum: "Worry Doll," "Polyphony," "Desert Song," "Old and Lost," "Bookmark"

Texas Poetry Calendar(s): "West Houston: Light Over Neighborhood," "Texas Photos: Osan AB, 1969"

Illya's Honey: "To Texas and Beyond," "Projection," "Tonality," "Backyard Laptop"

FreeFall - Canada's Magazine of Exquisite Writing: "Yellow-Blue"

Houston Poetry Fest Anthology 2013: "Lithuanian Elegy"

di-vêrse'-city 2013 (anthology of the Austin International Poetry Fest): "Weekdays"

Words & Art, Rice University Gallery: "El Pájaro," "Tree of Logos," "Houston Grandmaster," "Mudman Running"

Melancholy Hyperbole (melancholyhyperbole.com): "Flatland" and "Road Chant for a Mechanical Doll"

Friendswood Public Library website (*From the Reference Desk*): "Polyphony," "West Houston: Light Over Neighborhood": www.fplrefdesk.blogspot.com

Літературна Україна (Literary Ukraine) website: www.dikoepole.org/lu/index.php?a=showSingl&id=7

Contents, *Aching Miracle*

Contents continued, *Aching Miracle*

[1] *The Swan Princess* by Mikhail Vrubel, 1900.
The Tretyakov Gallery, Moscow, Russia. Oil on canvas.
Portrait of Nadezhda Zabela-Vrubel.

[2] Stylized detail of the monument in Donetsk, Ukraine,
commemorating Col. Franz Grinkevich, who commanded
the 32nd Guards Tank Brigade, one of the units that liberated
the city from Nazi occupation in 1943.

[3] *Six-winged Seraph* by Mikhail Vrubel, 1905.
Pushkin Memorial Museum, St. Petersburg, Russia.
Painting after Alexander Pushkin's poem, "The Prophet."

The Swan Princess [1]
[black-and-white]
by Mikhail Vrubel

Foreword

S ince the Moderns we have cultivated a fascination with gliding over impossible surfaces. The poet John Ashbery describes this movement as a realization that:

> the present moment may be one of an eternal series of moments, all of which will resemble it because, in some ways, they are the present, and won't in other ways, because the present will be the past by that time. [4]

The poetry of Elina Petrova presents a private emotional constant that withstands collapse by engaging mythologies of motion. With the kind of hyper-realistic grace that comes while watching figures present the illusion of distant speed or magnified slow motion, Petrova's poems solicit a literary courage that moves between lyric and elegiac verse.

Aching Miracle is filled with images of unresolved motion. Titles like "Green Boots," "Tibetan Slippers," "The Farther Shore," and an ekphrastic section entitled "Jogs at Rice Gallery" prepare the reader for a vehicle of enforced travel. This is not to imply that her work is a travelogue without contemplation, but that for all its geographical references — Texas, Louisiana bayous, Savannah, Donetsk, Lithuania, Gothenburg, and Nottingham, the Caribbean, Sinai, and Rome — readers will not find their discoveries on the Ukrainian Steppes or the Spanish Steps. Rather, as the volume progresses, the only landmark is a poet's voice in combat with loss and infatuated with the ironies of language.

We are given glimpses of a world linked and reeling in intimate collisions and abandonments: "Tiny people waved from porches of marshmallow / -roofed cottages to a train passing the Alps" (Worry Doll); "The world span — / the No-One's-Rose, a kaleidoscope / juggling with petal-splinters" (Tonality); "... his violin in the velvety sheath / with a sniper's rifle" (Maestro); a collision of J.M. Barrie, Patti Smith, and downtown Houston becomes "Fire, what have I done to you?" (Flatland); "... to the empty Ferris wheel / Shrouded with snow, black coal of waste banks" (Black Swans); "... but the gravestone could be one that Sherman's troops/ muddled up with drunken mischief" (Weddings of Bluffton, Cemeteries of Savannah); "... where Vikings won some battle, / at stuporous seniors slowly pushing walkers" (Reticent Saga); "The world buzzes like a remote toll road / or a wasp trying to get inside a light bulb" (Solar Winds); "Light / Shadow. Mozart's Adagio" (Road Chant for a Mechanical Doll); "Hidden life in puddles. He erases" (Mudman Running); "Ry Cooder's blues with a knife pressed on the string" (To Texas and Beyond). Throughout the volume the tropes of poetic language become juxtaposed with details of war, cultural vagrancy, and the reticent intransigence of existence.

"Road Chant for a Mechanical Doll" explores a barnacled surface of mobility at freeway speed. The poem reveals a moment of self-recognition amid annoyingly slow traffic, Christian symbology, and the speaker's own eye appears as the Egyptian Eye of Horus in her rear view mirror, "... the Dodge in front / (swim, Ichthus, support the troops) / To the right, in the mirror, a focused eye/ squints / goggles — swings of mascara." These are not traffic coincidences, but miniature moments that the poet constantly travels into and out of, but never through. The poem interweaves Mozart with the internally rhymed "Light / shadow. Mozart's Adagio," a line that functions as a soothing psalm (the 23rd) as the poem resolves in the speaker's dissolution, "I am a stranger in my own family. / I am a sister to any stranger / when I'm needed. *Am I needed?*" The poem creates intimacy with the mechanics of grammar, the deft imagery of blinks, squints, goggles, sun-mills, and a phrase of Mozart to build, as the title implies, a mechanical doll. But it's a peculiar doll. This automaton is hardly a device designed to allow little princesses to sleep and dream pleasantly. Rather it moves itself with rapidity that belies the thousand intricate sprockets, starts and stops, but presents a quick trembling illusion of human motion bound to a somatic musical splinter. Its meaning is only found through the illusion of motion.

Similarly in "Kyoto Dolls": "In my bedroom mirror are two black-haired Kyoto dolls." The reader finds the intimacy of the speaker's bedroom haunted by the astonishing travels of twin dolls through Guadalcanal, an Eric Satie jazz version of Grand Central Station, a film noir cowboy movie, movie themes, and metempsychosis of wounded cats, all temporarily resolved when the speaker puts down her rucksack next to an unnamed "you" and announces it's time "to go home," and this brief domestication is enjambed with "In the mirror." Nothing rests for more than an instant in these poems.

In *Aching Miracle* the poems become a singular album of impossibly complicated travel. Memory brings loss, domestic felicity is in an inescapable fun house, and uncontrollable conflict is everywhere. In "At 3:00 A.M. Triptych — Easter Bukowski," the poet, tested by insomnia, collapses images from her war-ridden hometown with the same day's images of a picturesque roadside near Dallas, and finds cynical wisdom of denial from Charles Bukowski. In the war-inspired "Donetsk

Shortly" found earlier in the book, a young girl in glasses seems a thief, but instead slips money in a one-armed war veteran's pocket, "It's nothing. Buy a bouquet / for your Valentine."

In the gorgeous "*Zefiro Torna*," the speaker watching a film of a merciful murder contemplates love causing vulnerability — "coalified branches" and "creased gasp for breath," but she tipsily sings along with Monteverdi's madrigal, an ode to the gentle wind of the west, whose fresh breath brings back spring inspirations and the revival of love. She evokes the mighty Zephyr who knows the world of the living and the Underworld, but whose return brings back the courage to love: "Love is the water we must pay for," whose return once again celebrates life like Botticelli's *Primavera*.

In the closing poem "Glow," the poet reminds us, "What makes us human is not even eloquence, / but the sculpting of time in memories, / an invisible impulse developing its glow." She ends with the line, "light years between the stars," a unit of speed abbreviating distance, not time. The poetry of this volume offers its salvation in the poet's refusal to surrender to a fleeting world she finds she can neither restrain nor integrate into — rather, she speaks to us passing, crafting her language to appear as intimate as a conversation with a stranger on a plane. We forget we are strangers.

Elina Petrova's first volume of poems in English is as beautiful as watching a figure skater smoothly execute axel jumps and death spirals and then viewing a slow motion projection of the constant jarring and collisions of those sharpened blades appearing to glide.

D. E. Zuccone
writer and educator
Vice President, Public Poetry

Houston, Texas
May 2015

---

[4] "John Ashbery, The Art of Poetry No. 33," *The Paris Review*, Winter 1983, interview by Peter A. Stitt

ACHING MIRACLE

Polyphony

All that unites us is a chronicle of rays
and its mistranslations.
Moses depicted with horns by Michelangelo
for *San Pietro in Vincoli,*
but one example.
Then basics of quantum mechanics:
similar to the double-slit experiment,
thoughts strobe pearls of particles
through lonely pinholes to the screen
until they diffract, interfere —
now waves of interwoven patterns.
That's how you reach me in 6000 miles,
sit on the corner of my bed and sigh.
Floundering on the edge
shapes a soul more sensitive
than the skin on a burglar's fingers,
yet it's nothing to be proud of:
a goldfish sees ultraviolet and infrared light,
butterflies smell pheromones from miles away,
a half-centimeter medusa can be immortal
in the polyp state, if not eaten.
When I think of you, the cat gazes in awe
at something slightly above my head.
I'm too awestruck — by prebiotic chemistry,
the illusion of blue sky over white light,
I'm touched — by people carrying on
like the illegal roofer who sends every dime he earns
to his children in Guatemala,
embraces them on Skype, for five years.
Complex and simple,
all that unites us is a symphony
by the One who told Moses on Sinai,
You shall not see me.

Worry Doll

On Christmas I listened to Pope Francis
and a Texas pastor whose wife, as we speak,
has been for seven weeks in intensive care.
Both of them talked about the power of prayer —
how to light inner peace from the higher candle
and soar above circumstances. A massive
children's railroad hummed in the church lobby.
Tiny people waved from porches of marshmallow
-roofed cottages to a train passing the Alps.
Taller people snapped selfies with cellphones —
especially where the train on a flyover arrived
above plastic palms to the manger in Palestine.

So did I — mesmerized by snowflakes
and the promise of a delayed miracle.
Then I closed my eyes, and saw white antelopes
turning into nurses, walking soundlessly
in shoe covers into the ward of the pastor's wife
to fix her plastic tubes. The light was harsh.
I wished peace to every soul, at least oblivion
kinder than the snow that meekly dressed
stacks of pale bodies slit up in Bosnia one distant winter —
I thought of things I didn't mean to think this Christmas,
because my country split, and a million lighters
from night-to-night waved in the frosted square.

A little girl gave me her worry doll —
a tiny cloth doll, *muñecas quitapenas,*
to whom a child confided her unrequited prayers.
"Lay me under your pillow to have a good sleep" —
said the doll with the girl's squeaky voice,
and continued in my undertone,
"I shall splash your worries in the waterfall
iridescent with tears of others. I shall
bring your phoenix egg through winged gardens
to the solar navel of the baby-Earth
where all that worried you will become my poem."

Aching Miracle

Yellow-Blue

Oh vitality — a persistent static spark,
parkour, young love unsolved.
Shadows in Hyde Park are short,
unlike memories.
Down — daffodils, up — the blue
molecules of sunshine: I spring
ashamed of my childish joy
near the statue of Wellington,
2000 miles from Crimea,
where Ukrainian ships are besieged.
Officers, sailors — my penniless schoolmates
abandoned by what's left of the country —
swore no allegiance to the Russian flag.
Dignity makes the family pantry empty
like the souls of those who compromise.
I found a pass to avoid the choice:
a passport — a blue heart transplant
for my second life, in which I watch
tourists snapping photos of ladies
in whimsical hats through the grill
at Buckingham Gates; I leap happily
in Hyde Park, with a lopsided
setter I named Iggy Pop.
Yellow-lipped daffodils,
drunken sapphire sky — colors
of the flag, fading with the peninsula
on the contoured map of my childhood.

Lithuanian Elegy
— for my mother, Galina Petrova

Irretrievable sunsets floated above pine trees,
through lily pads on a Lithuanian lake:
swelled with wet lilacs, watercolor streaks —
sunshine lava from afar, where crossroads turned mauve
and the first lightning flashed on the horizon.
A cascade of freshness, life itself
plunged into the vortices of brown irises:
our eyes reflected light so alike
until the days they peered at the last door —
white, with lackluster-violet shadows
looming for you that I couldn't find.

Puncture without anesthesia
is a grove with flickering stems and seconds:
twigs, bare twigs ...
people, unremarkable people
in mustard-yellow raincoats
rustle leaves underfoot, hasten away
to the railway platform.

It was a window behind the head of your bed,
and a vacuum-flask;
festered expanses of gaping sunsets,
the birch and withered grass.
You asked what was there. I lost
human words — lowed like Quasimodo.
Lightning or neon — something unclear
strobed in the vent duct in your ward.
"More Omnopon?"

· · ·

Aching Miracle

A shaky handwriting in your notepad,
"Happy birthday, my love.
After the eighth shot, I still remember."
Head of the hospice —
Charon with pensive horse eyes —
always knew in advance
when the next bed would become empty,
but would scarcely tell, when we would see again
silent, illuminated evenings near the green lake.

My unvoiced Hosanna ...
We would never be so hard-hearted,
seeing each other with eyes of Beyond.
Ashes of my candle-burned black locks
                              are the token
on the lapel of your new white suit.
Now I swim to you
                with my boyish haircut,
                      when I fall asleep.

Desert Song

River of my life carried you carefully,
pushed away to the safer shore
like the infant Moses.
Clouds floated in — orange-grey, feather-soft —
deep monastic voices.
Sinai of your eyes — wolfy-green, nomad-ochre —
spiraled into pupils.
Crust on hearts peeled to pulp — tannin-rich Carmel wines,
Black Arabian horses.

Ashtrays of the last nights. Before work
my high heels clicked at 5 a.m.
on the wet boulevards.
When I left our windswept rented flat,
walls with photos of your wife — proper
like lukewarm coffee on her empty table
between your business trips —
the inside of your ring bore the old
inscription, "This too shall pass."
I decorated my Christmas tree
with the bulbs of your promises,
and took it away — dry and prickly — in May.
I looked for you, and did not find you.
But I could leave the past like the bus
with any kind-hearted stranger
and start living, because — they say —
love is rather the house built with own hands,
than misled ganglia
at the Garden of Earthly Delights
and various soapy songs.

• • •

Aching Miracle

After cutting my light and flesh from yours,
anyone — more or less adequate in this solitary world —
could request my love and body
like that Bedouin in holey cross trainers
who pulled my hand up the last
icy steps to Mount Sinai,
wrapped me — before dawn — with a camel rag,
brought a cup of the Red
Sudan Rose tea against my hangover,
and said, "Stay with me under these stars
till we lose our last teeth —
you're a beautiful daughter of the desert."
I put a mint on his palm.
The first rays slit terracotta boulders
from the summit, where we stood,
down to Saint Catherine's gorge.
A pilgrim behind us sang in Greek.
My palms pulsated
with the sun in its excess.
I wasn't coming home — the world
was getting warmer without you.

To Texas and Beyond

She laid down between the rails
watching the vast train
whistle by — high above —
overloaded with cargo:
a clash of compartments, fumes
from the firebox of its sepia predecessor,
Ry Cooder's blues
with a knife pressed on the string,
the smell of fodder.
She got on that train:
a time traveler, peering
into swishing prairies,
the Tahoe-blue eyes of smudgy
short-tempered settlers
not yet sleekened into plankton
in district courts.
She believed in self-defense.
She believed in silence,
horse whispering, shingles
of southbound nomads
more than in justice —
gore at the sheepfold,
dusted with snow
labor camp landfills
of her forefathers.

Projection

In the other world
her touch is a gentle surf —
a warm splash of hands.
Her laughter
chimes without cracking.
Under her eyelids
the lime-green sun
pulses its dilated pupil.
The morning
smells like a rain-washed apple,
her infant's skin,
cheek-to-cheek
after the war-long parting.
In the other world
she remembers
why she awakes.

Tonality

When you realize there is nothing lacking ... — Lao Tzu

There is not much to wish for beyond
what is currently here — early
afternoon in the backyard,
a patio table under an oak,
wind shifting sun splashes
on the red bird-house.
I have loved people in love
since I was a sick girl, often —
with a compress at my throat —
smiling out the window at boys
carrying schoolbags for my girlfriends,
who forgot to visit me. The word "own"
never passed my lips. The world span —
the No-One's-Rose, a kaleidoscope
juggling with petals-splinters
of the shell-shocked heart. After
many dead years, and years alive
near the dying, each day is splendid —
the longed-for water from cupped hands,
or that slow, crystal movement
from Mozart's 23rd, where the swift
fingers of Horowitz hover low over the keys —
swallows before rain, passing
a scrolling text from subtler frequencies.

• • •

A semitone is the most dissonant
when it sounds harmonically, yet
the options are thrilling. Whether we sip
one martini with two straws, whether
I choose red-flesh tomatoes at fresh
markets of the Gulf Coast, or a ticket
to East Ukraine where smoke
from roadblocks eddies up to a jet —
as long as tonality is true,
there is not much lacking.

Timeline

Backyard Laptop, Texas

Honeysuckle and Thai spice
waft from behind the fence.
Gravel sparkles quartz-white
on my cat's burial place.
A red cardinal brings me to tears
with the intensity of his beauty.
Perhaps, it's not even about him
but a wish to caress the day
at low tide: calm, lukewarm
like Gulf foam at four p.m.
when my timeline bursts —
the blood pump with news
from East Ukraine, where
I left my father.

Donetsk Shortly

I

A mortar shell explodes
five hundred feet from the minibus
thumping a love song on a Russian
radio station. A cigarette falls
from the driver's hand onto the snow.
Women squinching on worn corduroy seats
stare at a tiny icon of Saint Nicholas
swinging from the windshield. A four-
year-old clutches her mom's sleeve: "If
we ask God to turn off the war, will he?"

II

When shrapnel pierced
the shoulder of her frayed coat
she was standing in the soup kitchen line
murmuring about her pension
they stole after she'd worked sixty years
in a Ukrainian chemical plant,
about her late husband's photos
she couldn't find under crumbled
sheetrock in the living room
bombed last Tuesday.

III

He is back from the scorched-black
snowy debris of Donetsk airport.
In a Kiev subway a girl in glasses
slips fifty hryvnas into his pocket.
One-armed, he catches her hand.
She hugs him. "Take it, dear —
it's nothing. Buy a bouquet
for your Valentine."

Maestro

For six months he's been missing.
They called him Maestro
for his violin in the red velvet sheath
with a sniper's rifle.
The short, lean bundle
of tanned muscles, a knowing grin,
charcoal focused eyes —
an unruly patriot, a problem
for government officials.
Jailed before the Maidan revolution
for disturbing the peace
of corrupt Kiev,
he fled to Prague, but returned
when war stirred. If only
he hadn't talked to journalists
about money stolen from the battalion
fighting on provisions from villagers,
about front-line officers shot in the back,
but not by the enemy.
Fellow-soldiers last saw him before
the dispatch of the afternoon train.
Plainclothes men swiftly picked up
his tarpaulin bag and violin case,
shoved him — with bound hands —
to the car with tinted windows.
I last saw him at dawn
in a dream. Maestro cut
a slice from a ripe watermelon
and handed it to his little son.
It was sunny. No artillery noise.
A red-breasted bird
under the balcony whistled
a theme by Paganini.

Old and Lost

If they start to go over the cliff — I mean if they're running
and they don't look where they're going, I have to come
out from somewhere and catch them. That's all I'd do all
day. I'd just be the catcher in the rye. — J. D. Salinger

Days slip between my fingers — meticulously shaped acrylic tips
without which I'd bite cuticles to blood. Autumnal light throbs
through me addicted tenderness to a shortening life, tempts me to
sprawl out — untanned, blue-vein topless — on the mowed yard.

"I got so much more, so much more love left to give," Marianne
Faithfull sings with a cracked voice to her early film, *The Girl on a Mo-*
torcycle. Oh freckled, fertile/sterile, many-breasted/flat-chested Isis
in the leather suit. My Krav Maga trainer jokes: one day you have en-
ergy to repel a regiment, the next you tumble like a depleted tire.

Have you driven from Houston along Interstate 10? On the way to
Beaumont, there are greenish, shallow bayous that feed the Trinity
River. When it's dry, they evaporate. When it's rainy, they flow —
the Old and Lost Rivers.

I recall a white blur — a doctor in the emergency room who checked
my pupils, dilated after two hundred pills hidden in the school pen-
cil case until I took them all at once. "I won't report you to a psy-
chiatrist, because at sixteen you're more thoroughgoing than I —
just haven't learned to compromise, haven't met someone to talk to."

In that haze, unfocused sunny dust waltzing around a plastic bottle
with physiological saline, I forgot to ask his name, but for many years
he was the one who talked to me, kept my hand when I balanced on
the tarred edges of high-risers' roofs, looking down at anthills of children building and crashing castles in the courtyard sandbox.

Here I am, past sixty. Child therapist, Old and Lost like those brack-
ish rivers in Chambers County. Still trying to find a flow, a red fish
in Trinity Bay. Keeping up hands for others. A catcher in the rye.

Aching Miracle

West Houston:
Light Over Neighborhood

At the hour of slack lounge chairs
and monotonous rotor blades
of a sheriff's chopper circling,
colors become so intense
that tarnished driveways
glow like schist with apricot grains,
lawns float, unreal emerald,
through a pink haze of crape myrtles.
Garages are open: in a doorway
a neighbor stands in his shorts only —
a stout question mark
with a glass of carmine Thai tea.
The off-white, rheumy-eyed cat
walks through the quiet street and wails,
demanding his portion of tenderness.
Everything spellbound by last dabs of light
looks chokingly mortal
in its ordinariness.

Texas Photos: Osan AB, 1969
— for my friend, Arnold Henry

Better he'd gotten out of that bayou place
to not chase the hoodoo his daddy chased —
muck himself up in the Woodstock mud,
hit the road.
Then who would surface farm roads, fix the cars,
who'd buy a cabin for his sloe-eyed gal
when she gets pregnant?

Far from her cornfield near the old oil rig,
he wiped bony hands with a soiled rag,
smiled at lifers:
hairy torsos dismissed to Osan —
a softball tossed beside the airbase barn
housing a missile.
He gazed at these noisy, coarse men
and muttered thanks
for bringing 'em all from Nam.

Aching Miracle

Weekdays

When you win a case after months of a research
that no one would do better than you, but are left unpaid,
you come home, brown eyes darker than usual,
almost apologetic, downcast as if you deceived
the old dream of a house: the fireside, the terrace
where you'd breathe in spruce air while I read to you
my book with not one sad poem in it — the house
we would finally bring children in from afar,
where they need us as much as we need them,
to share a warm afternoon filled with a glow
like a glass of strawberry juice, pierced with the sunbeam.

And when you still stand lingering with a tie in your hand,
the lump in my throat is nothing but tenderness.
I embrace you. Your racing thoughts hush.
We stand still, smolder as two candles melting together,
and then smile, move on to a dinner that's never scant.
Lulled by bustles of a three-piece-suited hero on the screen,
we cave in darkness, holding on to hands as if we were
life rafts for each other, shipwrecked, or stitched
plush puppies left over after the Valentine sale.

Flatland

He was a poet; and they are never exactly grown-up.
— J.M. Barrie, *Peter Pan in Kensington Gardens*

Captain Hook, I fed your hand to a crocodile
not out of malice, but for survival.
This city is swollen with oil. Towers
are eerie at night — gators never sleep.
Your clocks tick away in the crocodile paunch.
Birds guide the flyers.
Even disheveled-grey *à la* Patti Smith,
no one owns a watch in the Neverland.

I hover — a firefly way up over dim lofts, lounges —
along a procession of headlights in a traffic trance,
I steep-dive under the bridge to Chenevert Street
where the hungry lost boys line up on Sundays:
the ceaseless shrill of a highway junction,
gapped teeth, macaroni & cheese I serve
warm styrofoam in chapped hands.
In the mornings I shoot upwards
peering at people who peer at numbers,
shove through cramped cubicles
with hope for advancement
like lobsters with the tied up claws
in the aquarium of a seafood restaurant.

Everyone was a winged child. Everyone is ...
This is my neighborhood: middle-aged,
neatly mowed, no more anticipations —
anxious doves at pink-ash dawns. Flatland.

Each day is the future —
firm fresh fruit I make juice, pour
into your glass on the glass table
with a familiar sunray trembling.
October air is brisk, intense. Judgments
are softer, passions — tender, detached:
embrace too much to claim possessions.
Fairy tales ... Maples in flame send firebirds.
Fire, what have I done to you?

Aching Miracle

Tuesday Afternoon in Texas

The afternoon is calmly
overcast and cozy
before first large raindrops
steam on the asphalt paths
and then the bebop starts —
Coltrane's "Love Supreme" of trickles
that beat down on the windows
like fingers on the brass.

A lazy afternoon —
all move in slow motion:
cops gnaw late barbecue
and drivers step on brakes
before a 60-IQ
inmate in a Huntsville gurney
will be injected with
the final, lulling dose.

A drowsy afternoon,
impassive like a jury
who wait for lunch recess
while coffee perks in vain,
and Nguyen across the street
files nails of endless clients
and watches crime news all day,
not foreseeing the rain.

Weddings of Bluffton,
Cemeteries of Savannah

The cutting edge is up. They walk down
the church steps through the Arch of Sabres.
The tall lily-bride: a shy droop of her shoulders,
"No returns" — her CEO daddy's mantra.
The groom: Captain's uniform in blue,
his sister's concealer on the black eye
the bride gave him the stag-night before.
Last year in Iraq, his boyish face grew thinner,
the crow's feet more pronounced.
The Italian priest almost made him tearful.
I still see the newlyweds through *sfumato* —
sun haze softening borders of light-and-shade
with sepia smoke round the bridal posy,
and I can't unsee the plot developed —
the groom's sister's quilt stitched for six months
to be presented at the wedding party,
but not welcomed: "Poor thing," valerian
drops for the women of the house.
Each piece of the motley quilt
from another state, another relative.
Shall this too pass?

Clouds shape fast: sables with pearly undercoats,
lucent-eyed gaps in Renaissance ceiling
painted on the way. Heart of the wise
teaches his mouth, makes it silent,
when his words aren't a honeycomb.
Before picking up more guests from the airport,
we stop at Savannah Cemetery, read inscriptions.
Spanish moss trails its dreadlocks to the tombs.

• • •

Aching Miracle

Here's the poet-duelist shot through the heart
by another in the regiment, his only friend.
The epitaph says the nature of the quarrel is unknown,
but the gravestone could be one that Sherman's troops
muddled up with drunken mischief.
What's known is the road where the duelist's hearse
passed the arch of live oaks with grey moss earrings
was as eerily scenic as the one we drove
to the wedding, and that Spanish moss obtains
nutrients from the air and rains — an epiphyte,
a rootless poet of Southern Gothic tales.

Needle

Birch leaves tremble in sunlight.
Their veined, freckled amber
frames the sky tondo.
Skin glows at the longed-for touch
on Kirlian photos.
Caritas abundat in omnia,
and it's piercing, bracing —
the air I'm still in, a flicker
on the screen of the world
I know no better than a nun,
following with her eyes
people encapsulated in SUVs —
busy, passing, passing busy.

He knew human nature deep
inside out, to an overdose.
The actor my age, found
prone on his bathroom floor
in West Village:
two envelopes with "Ace of Spades,"
the needle as a need
for happiness — synecdoche.
I watch a fragment with him
singing "Slow Boat to China"
and I wish instead of rehab
he went East, unhurriedly
restoring to a source of needling
sympathy, and joy poured out for free
in the air, intravenously like the sun
corpuscles in a bloodstream.

. . .

Aching Miracle

Caritas abundat in omnia ...
"We saw Phil with the kids yesterday
in the coffee shop. He smiled,"
neighbors tell a police officer.
"Nothing connects to anything else,"
mutters the flabby hero on the screen
to a drug dealer,
"All my parts don't add up to one ...
to one me."

Black Swans

Black swans I fed as a child.
The white seemed plumper, untroubled,
with a virtuous family bearing —
unlike those entwined
arcs of the longer, visibly thinner necks
with an intense obsidian sheen,
a concealed fragility of rare species.

White parks I roamed in my youth.
Cold bark of poplars. Fresco-blue
smoke eddied from huts in the ravine
to the empty Ferris wheel.
Shrouded with snow, black coal of waste banks.
Crumbs of rye bread spilled to albino crows.
Fresh tracks unseen. The thin ice crust
on the warm milk of life.

My joyless neighbors, why
life made you sting each other with words
rather than sing, like gondoliers
to the olive gold of the old lagoon —
be it the slush on the roadside
of my coal-miner town, or the remote sky —
the feverish Abyssinian turquoise,
for Arthur Rimbaud's sake?

• • •

Aching Miracle

I sung alone. To the black swans,
to Tesla's pigeon at the hotel window,
to Glenn Gould's low chair,
to the rusted bus in Alaska
where the young tramp died
by eating the wrong berries.
All kinds of solitude
seemed to me more bearable
than the day-to-day decay
of what might keep people together,
not like geese paired for breeding,
or peasants — for coping with sour times,
but for subtler reasons.
For cutting the rope
like a mountain climber
who dangled and finally had to
rely on someone else's pull,
for a shimmer, a sheer chiffon
flying above entwined hands
falling into Bach partitas.

Cadenza

And what is left: the empty sky of Carthage
above the final columns tumbled to the clay?
Spilled on the dazzling slab of marble,
the turquoise beads — Dido's lament
                                "Remember me"?
Or tachycardia of the cadenza
played on the harpsichord to dripping icicles
in the vacated town of my youth's
infatuations left in the burn unit of the past?

In concert halls my thoughts float eastward —
to the doorpost, where we once leaned
and lingered to turn the key for half an hour
while kissing in greatcoats hoary with frost,
to frescos on the high ceiling we whirled under,
amid the leaf-fall of unblessed spirits
in my remote plundered country —
decayed empire with the change of seasons
as the only news relieving. Phantom
causalgia of amputees is not a testimony,
but there are rosaries of pavement with
every pebble and red leaf remembered,
the photon glow which remains in place
of missing branches, the bodiless powers.

All points on the circle of time are equidistant.
All follies are still happening, light years
are multiplying chlorophyll in foliage.
The Sun chrysanthemum still throbs and captivates.
This shall not pass — the living island floats
like Kitezh with invisible domes chiming
and people visiting the hermitage of my dreams.
I set the table for them and do not shun
the other-worldly shine of their presence.
The ghost spaceship of the subconscious passes
through tunnels of alternative timelines,

                                    • • •

Aching Miracle

cadenzas of tender days, clear-obscure
in fidgety oblivion full of warmth and voices.
Then days flash by under the ancient sky.

Green Boots

All my ardent mishandled stories
healed by writing in Russian,
clear my caches.
Cleanse me with hyssop and I'll be clean.
Wash me and I'll be whiter than snow
or tungsten wire, whiter than my kimono
frayed by sparring and the raked ashes
of scarlet charcoals I fire-walked
on a Texas ranch.

He saved the green boots
I wore the day he arrived in Kiev ...
Fuzzy sunbeams caressed the lengthy bridges
drifting in sleepy traffic from the airport.
He held my warm hand bashfully
when onion-shaped domes shone through fog,
and the whole ancient city on auburn-green hills
between the wing-beats of two silvery rivers
appeared, dazzled, resounded as a fugue
in old Slavonic polyphonies.
We left heavy bags and strolled paved streets
like long-separated siblings who couldn't
talk enough. We moved from one café to another
illuminated capsule in floating twilight drizzle,
then lingered in the kitchen, blowing at midnight tea.
Jet-lagged, charmingly short-sighted
in outdated glasses
through which he saw only goodness in me,
he would protect me
even against my own tongue.
His unfeigned kindness touched and carried me
130 degrees West & 20 degrees South
towards new latitudes.

The Song of Ascents

Like a flower wilted in a bud
glued with fungus,
like a body aged not knowing
the strength of its muscles,
like a glowing charcoal of ecstasies
thrown to the ashpit of prudency —
like everything that I don't want
to be, but still am, I long for you
to strike the bright match of me.

Cowboy's Horse

The black horse tethered to a tree
with his head lifted.
Glassy eyes dry out tears with the sky.

Aching Miracle

The Farther Shore

Sun-dappled horses,
field flowers in forelocks,
eyes, honey-brown like mine,
only larger, pensive

let me press my temple
to your shiny neck,
a stranger's horse,
let me untether you

waltz you round
while the sun is high —
we're both from a dream
someone questioned.

Who's talking? Old souls:
we saw *Killing Fields*,
passed barbwire in silence —
crickets & barrage mines

family photos left behind —
wilted magnolia leaves.
Does fate intend some tie
between us two?

Farther Shore, I came
without knick-knacks, no
more sanity-bound, free
like your Horse Spirit.

Tibetan Slippers

*We could hold conversations entirely without ever opening
our mouths. She called it 'shining.'* — Stephen King

These are red Tibetan slippers
I bought in Haight-Ashbury.
My Maine Coons gnaw at
the yellow-green embroidery sewn
over discounted genuine leather.
The ornament reminds me of Green
Tara and bodhisattvas whose images
I browsed in encyclopedias
from the sickbed of my childhood —
when icicles, Flemish paintings,
inflamed tonsils, and a blaze
of morbid Slavic books I'd read so early
they seemed a prelude to the day
I would go to far and wondrous places
in the New World and the Himalayas,
where I had to adopt a child
as lost and beaming as me.
And we would be shining.

Aching Miracle

Lightweight

To remain in the light body —
merely ribcage guarding, uncushioned
with airbags of riches and notions
borrowed from hefty folios.
To act obnoxiously unreasonable —
leap over obstacles with your grandchildren,
prefer the scattered solar plasma of joy
to synthesis, change the name again,
a tongue, a syntax of poems that can't be foreign,
bring you to learn breathing at the Mount Song.
To tear along the freeway to the widening sky —
swift cumulus clouds in sideview mirrors,
quadrophonic Pink Floyd and long
undyed hair lashing against a smile.

Orlando

I used to give my bread and wine to them
like to the guests sent from beyond,
to crash against the cursed questions ...
as if complying with the ironies
suggested here / now, would be a sellout;
as though encapsulated in a teenage body
something in me would wear varying fates
like Woolf's *Orlando*.
A century and sex — they scarcely matter:
the same naïve infatuations, myths
and countries that whizz by.
Will I get wiser closer to autumn?
Just grant me a lingering in my belated spring.
Like a sleepwalker in my white, timeworn kimono
I leave the bokken sword and dance
my Butoh to translucent cherry blossoms
that reaches the absent — sensed, but invisible,
and earthly ecstasies — sublimed, yet unspent.

From the Terrace

At 3 a.m., when sheep are counted
along with fundamentally insolvable,
yet not overgrown problems,
there is a light field for drifting,
reinventing Eden with the flawed
ripe apple of the heart. Perhaps,
curtains flying to the terrace in Rimini,
August, the curvature of two
tired swimmers against the sun —
clingy like Francesca & Paolo, divine
and comic as lovers commonly are —
elongated shadows on pebbles
which the calming surf warms with foam.
Melancholy in the form of conic cypresses,
emptying piazzas, arcades: all
that matters
is music —
antimatter
for a recurring
dream.

Ultima Thule

At 3 a.m., when sheep are counted
along with pieces taken from a chessboard
(unlearned pawns, a decapitated bishop
of the motherland, mother-queen that perished
not even moving from her white square)
there is a boat on blinding waters,
my frozen hands which used to dip into fish,
pull out gills with no knife, build
a house on four winds, with the cornerstone
three times knocked with a mallet ...
Far from the colony, a seagull woman
squeals lullabies to the village dunce
who has been the kindest to her.
A little girl and a husky-dog smile
when we meet at dunes,
shine through me from the depth
of their blue-crystal eyes,
and I know that some
calm and flaxen day
they will come for me.

Easter Bukowski

At 3 a.m., with no sheep left to count
under the tremor of my eyelids (along
with tank-spotting — armored troop
carriers passing my street in Ukraine)
I see the road: a flicker
of asphalt gravel at sunset,
patches of orange Indian paintbrushes
mixed on-the-run with bluebonnets,
an exit to the sleek frowning skyline
next to baptism in the stock tank
at a cowboy church; Denny's
with all-you-can-eat-pancakes
for the poor-tipping guests of La Quinta.
Wherever you stop, life is abundant,
if you stay — as Bukowski said —
far enough from the human race.
So do I — pull over to feel alive,
then drink myself to sleep.

Reticent Saga

Haakan owns a sterile, neatly shelved house in Noll —
Nil, or whatever they call
        that snow-heaped settlement near Göteborg,
where lonely-drinking neighbors
                            peep through hobbit windows,
and crispy bed sheets become cubistic,
                            drying in barren yards.
(Entrance: a smudgy low cliff with
        a clumsy notice "HOLLYWOOD"
                    painted at night by bored pranksters.)

Haakan is a tall, natty Export Director.
                        Twice-divorced. At times sentimental.
Ladies from Eastern Europe sent him epistles
                        that March in the hospital
when we browsed the family albums
                        for his dad, a physicist
who happened to hold my hand
                        with his last Hennessey
and joke that his shadow tried to joke with me after all.

The sequence of that day buzzes like a live fly
                    in the amber of my remembrance.
There the last morphine hisses.
We cling to each other with an anonymous nurse,
                        both sobbing in "Svenska."
A deranged seagull bumps again,
                    against the vast vestibule window.

                                        • • •

Haakan's family chooses
          an exquisite restaurant for the funeral repast.
His mother buys a wide-brimmed hat for horse racing
                  and new napkin-holders.
His brother's bold-headed girlfriend
          dons her Harley Davidson's helmet.

Then I stare at moving sunbeams
          on the bricks of Vadstena fortress,
at the piercing blueness of a cold lake
          where Vikings won some battle,
at stuporous seniors slowly pushing walkers
          and spray-tanned moms
                rocking their baby strollers.
A distant ship hoots. I foresee
a long drive with the reticent stranger,
                a fiancé-not-to-be —
several red wooden barns
          snowbound in windy wastelands.

Nottingham Roots

He licked the éclair off my fingers
        and said I was gorgeous,
"A gorgeous sad fish without water.
                No ambitions."
I thought I was the water
absorbing men's stories I'd rather not fish for,
            but, once saw, cared.

Once at sixteen, Edward Jr. "the Third,"
a lean, "four-eyed" competitive runner,
        ran away from his despotic
           theologian father in Nottingham.
He picked crumbs in Parisian bistros
        from plates he washed
           and interpreted *nouveaux riches*
until he reached Cambridge,
        staged his play on campus,
           made some German pregnant
and moved to sleek Frankfurt suburbs
           without her.

No curtains.
The alarm-clock would shriek at five.
A new PhD wife from St. Petersburg
           played the piano,
but preferred to sell jewelry
           at the remote airport,
while his screams, "*Scheiße!*"
        exorcized his translators till late evenings.
Then Opera. Tuxedo dinners.
        She collected Art Deco,
           and insisted to make love kiss-free.

       . . .

Now she lives under his storey and stalks his girls:
some of them, "stray foreign scum," clatter
their heeled hooves on the mosaic parquet
                              she cherished,
and fling bottles to a wrong trash can.
Edward favored the book prize
                    with his own name
and finally visited parents
              he planned to see with me.

His mother still plays that cello.
Dad watches TV:
apathetically, all day long,
on the loudest volume,
and shuffles in knitted socks.
His eyes look rheumy.
And he doesn't criticize
anybody
anymore.

Sunflower

The train accelerated. Gust from the window
cross-hatched with my hair. Anonymous rivers,
lopsided lampposts and hovels, birches —
twigs pleading in sign language flashed by.
Smokers banged on doors at the entryway,
bringing smells of the sour communal past
into a corridor where the conductor
in flaked make-up clinked, handing
tea-glasses in laced aluminum holders.

My neighbor, somewhat rugged for his forties,
not yet bald, soft-spoken, looked livelier before
his little son leaned out of the compartment.
The boy's unwinking blue eyes smiled.
Straw-yellow hair ruffled his round
large head. I thought, *Sunflower*.
His father glanced with aloof disenchantment
at that large head, not of his family line:
"At seven, he can't read simple words."

The boy stood close, blushing, then held
onto the window handrail, fanned his face
with the breeze from the darting sea of grass,
chirped to himself in Ukrainian with a comic
intonation that reminded me of my grandma.
He sounded wiser than us, at least more curious
about what passed on his movable screen.
I stole him for a stroll down the aisle, grabbed
a newspaper for a game of magic headlines.

• • •

Beetles and butterflies of letters broke
into a dance of syllables. "Radar! Racecar!"
Repeated by the boy and read with my voice
in reverse, syllables rose to words —
we yelled them, sang, until a sentence
became a field we walked through freely,
quickening our steps,
spitting husks of sunflower seeds;
stiffening into scarecrows
with straw-stuffed heads
only if strangers come near.

Campari

Loaded with Bitter Campari,
in a Caribbean swim-up bar,
harder than Nicolas Cage
in the Desert Song Motel,
she heals. Her eyes squint
at the edge of violet tiles
merged into turquoise oblivion.
Catamarans vanish
in an unintelligent,
volatile sea of Blue Curacao.
Soft ivory sand wiped of memories.
Bleeding pages of her Slavic ancestry
give fewer paper cuts.
A new name picks her randomly:
Xue Tao, Mrs. Jones, a featherbrained
señorita 36-26-36
floating in weightlessness
with a carmine drink.
Now she can't recollect the day
when landing
in her coal-mine hometown
became less soothing than take-offs —
just condensate
that again streams rapidly
across her airplane window
and Nina Simone's remix
"I'm feeling good."

Tundra Wildflowers

On peaks of the Rocky Mountains life is timid,
taught by piercing winds not to stand out —
grow in width, to depth,
turn a half-inch face to the sun
and store nutrients in six-foot roots.
Any tiny yellow Aven is an immigrant
whose depth remains unnoticed.

Solar Winds

Don't judge a man out of context.
His work is the context — something solar
in veins with Renaissance vigor.
At night we are different. Vulnerable.
Warmth-seeking trespassers
knocking at dreams of each other. Naked.
The world buzzes like a remote toll road
or a wasp trying to get into a light bulb.
Monotony slides to visions
fitfully streaming through miles.

You are older now. Wrinkles
only set off the shine of eyes.
You bring me a flower — the rosy-
yellow bud I planted for you that spring
still blossoms in its dual alchemy.
Hank's *"Kaw-liga"* crackles
through a weakening signal
of a country radio station.
I kiss your forehead, while your dry
lips are in fever for more.
My husband sighs, seeks after me again
in his nightmare, turns to cocoon in blankets
before the workday in courtrooms.
My dream lingers, though.
I see a lone ear of wheat
and make you describe its gold
light-and-shade time-lapses
in the morning, at noon,
in the soft remains of the day.
My solar battery goes off-scale,
juxtaposed with visions of many
people I cannot cease caring for.

· · ·

Aching Miracle

Lack of melatonin, my brain
craves for a milky, moon-pale
sedative Yin to dim the flare.
When I say this, the Moon waxes —
I see her slowly rotating counterclockwise,
with a shy geisha smile.
The warm Earth is spinning,
waving with tall pine trees,
as if they were algae swaying under the water.
Dandelions of memories scatter
transparent seeds where the passage of time
is no more tangible.

Solar winds rock me to heavier sleep ...
You sit at the threshold.
Wheat. Timeless tenderness.
My neighbor starts mowing his grass at dawn.
Don't judge the man out of context.

Zefiro Torna

I'm not concerned about turbulence —
the cold silver of jet flaps
concealed at an angular velocity,
a swollen blue streak,
a farewell ray sunk in a glass-wool strati
like a sliver of orange peel in Viennese coffee.
Decadent blood.
A blonde steward pours more Burgundy —
his gelled hair, tangential fan of crow's feet
nears to the Monteverdi in my headphones:
Zefiro Torna ...

Amour lights the screen
omitting subtitles when Jean-
Louis Trintignant — a retired piano teacher —
suffocates his bedridden wife with a pillow
out of pity, adorns her with petals.
I know his feeling.
You wouldn't do it for me, and it's a shame.
In every tavern we dined,
you bought from street vendors
a long-stemmed, laboriously revived rose —
an old maid on her wedding day.

What is love after all —
Egon Schiele's creased gasp for breath?
Your chevalier patience for coalified branches
that start blooming in me again?

· · ·

It may be beyond us —
under clouds we skim on —
where tarpaulins collect rainwater,
five-year-old Nishimwe
walks to the Kigali market
with a tin jar to fill, but water is costly.
Love is the water we must pay for.

Zefiro Torna — return, oh Zephyr.
With the gentle motion of your butcher hands
scatter the grasses in waves —
I am in shambles: now I weep, now I sing.

The Holiday Season

makes me daydream about caribou
stiffened in astonishment
at the misty frozen river,
about hiking snowy hills
with my heart hovering in silence.

A nightmare non-stop family reunion,
blood ties tightening: people cooking,
"fixing," snapping at toast while talking.
I'm caught staring at a blue jay
out the misted bay window —
choked on coffee.
Tell me more about your sister who joined a cult
and, when asked which church she went to,
she kicked her momma's dishwasher —
it puffed black smoke.
They tell me. I translate every word
for my father, then drive him to a three-hour
mass with the Russian diaspora that chants
after Patriarch Cyril, "Crimea is ours!"
but confesses only lesser wrongs
under the priest's brocade omophorion.
I confess that during mass my mind
drifted to sex, and that I stash
seasonal joys away from the family
by escaping to Barnes & Noble
where my open-wiring seeks silence,
that slow electricity disperses in blood
like the gentle tannins of Pinot
or the first movement of Samuel
Barber's violin concerto.

. . .

It's 40 degrees and rains ceaselessly.
A hooded man in the worn bookstore armchair
snores, departing from an even pitch
like a broken compressor.
At the table behind me, a stocky lady
in a sweatshirt *comenta las ventas*
on her speakerphone, while a grey
Indian nurse — also on a cellphone —
asks someone gently whether his patient
slept better last night.
He coughs, deep and dry, reads the same
Haruki Murakami novel that I read.

We are not linked in harmonies,
but through wounds, noise.
The homeless hooded man twitches
as if he dreamt he was a battered dog
who skidded trying to flee.
And I daydream. Hiking in silence
with a hovering heart, a charmed deer
in sparkling snow, a puff of pure breath.
Eyes speak truer than the tongue.
Canoe me as a river —
my rapids are deep, unpredictable,
tender to those they won't drown.

In Ten Minutes

McGovern Gardens are closing.
After another month without privacy,
I stare from the shade of the concrete
entry pavilion at fountains in the sun —
the pale-blue rectangular basin,
six low bubblers alternating a bullet shape
with an impressive launch of silver rockets.

Minimalistic chairs of red and grey.
Two in my corner are taken
by Chinese moms, silently watching
their well-behaved girls in sundresses
running from a distance. There
the waterfall cleaves a grassy hill
with spiral trails full of lingering guests.

Over a megaphone the caretaker thanks us
for leaving on time. My listless shiver
is not quite over. Fountains gush
with renewed force. Tears, involuntarily
as though there weren't mine,
stream down my cheeks.
I'm not even unhappy.

Flying Bow

Anima, Animus —
the shadow of man in me,
the shadow of me in man.
A stretched string,
bow without an archer —
with all my strength
I'm not whole
without your hands.

Couples on yoga mats
on AstroTurf
in Town & Country square
make me, who has
never been jealous, jealous.
My sun-ripe bodiness
follows their elevated push-ups.
The man's feet — pressed
against that soft area
between her hips and ovaries —
slowly turn her arched in midair.

The core strength: co-strength,
co-weakness — square abs
and a lack of hope shared
with a drinking companion.
Try with me "Flying Bow" —
make me hover for a child
I could give you.

Bookmark

My son, who I saw in the book of belated life,
though still haven't met, but I placed the bookmark — a red
maple leaf before your unread chapters — I won't
have much to teach you: a few books, kung fu kicks,
commandments that I failed to follow, the photo
of Gandhi's last sandals stored in my cellphone,
but I'll give you a key to the spacious room — You,
and I'll try to stay younger to watch you grow
so different from me, so adorably different.

My blood is too thin to pass heredity,
notice its discord with genetics of strangers —
random spirits exchanging warmth are family
while the sun stages the same antiquated play:
the raspberry plasma disc lifts from the grey
non-stop highways to white hot madness,
then descends into the lava-ocean — Hawaiian
orange-violet that turns into a bruise, then peace,
the twilight of the dove, unknown darkness.

What's invisible is the key:
you will learn to lift a little sun through your body —
from the golden stove of causes to the white
chrysanthemum bursting with a thousand limbic petals
above the skyline of the bayou city; you'll learn to exhale
through your palms to ground, hear the whispering pines,
notice that horses ask with the wet plums of their eyes.
I'll be there — just a bookmark, the red leaf in your life,
always with you, even after the book is closed.

Aching Miracle

Road Chant for a Mechanical Doll

Light / shadow. Light / shadow.
Live oaks. Mozart's Adagio,
the twenty third in A Major.
My turn signal blinks on the dashboard
only to hasten the Dodge in front
(swim, Ichthus, support the troops).
To the right, in the mirror, a focused eye
squints / goggles — swings of mascara.
A battered Camry cleaves across:
a pressure wave from loud bass,
the chrome sun-mill in spiked wheel rims.
The starched shirts. The Starbucks's cups.
The same old tramp who blesses for a buck.
We are moving. *Where am I moving?*
Light / shadow. Mozart's Adagio,
the twenty-third in A Major.
I am a stranger in my own family.
I am a sister to any stranger
when I'm needed. *Am I needed?*

Rain Pours

Andrés Orozco-Estrada — high
on caffeine before conducting Dvořák's 7th
in D minor — sleeks his wavy black hair
backstage at Stude Hall, changes the brown
Ralph Lauren shirt that doesn't match his pale
determined face. I wait outside, taking photos
from afar behind a stranger in black, resting
against the vertical aperture of James Turrell's
Twilight Epiphany — the grassy, truncated
pyramid's atrium under the illuminated
roof with clouds in its opening.
In my forties, I'm in a way sixteen —
the same sixteen when I thought I'd soon
meet someone who celebrates rain like I do,
that life should resist the adjective "lukewarm" —
the word Andrés teases his orchestra with
on rainy, unenthusiastic Mondays.
Drenched, I lean against a student's bicycle
to snap pictures, anticipating Andrés's
conducting fiesta — his grasshopper's leap
in the tight Nehru jacket, and that impulse
akin to my naïve, explosive happiness —
duende of cherry blossoms under swollen
graphite sky that rains into this poem
where the stranger in the atrium stares
at the courtyard of Rice's School
of Political Science; the woodwind section
straightens music stands for cross-rhythms
of Dvořák's furiant dance, and my hands
adjusting the objective lens at Epiphany
are wet, but never lukewarm.

Houston: Sea of Tranquility

At some point we drive to the grocers
in pajamas,
tired of pressing non-stop in district courts,
road bottlenecks, parties in starched shirts.
Sea of Crises.
At some point the distant gulf breath
purls into a moist
overcast twilight over bayou trails,
ripples olive-grey reflections in pools
of Tranquility Park near City Hall.
Steel cylinders tower in pale water —
seas of Moisture, Showers, walkways
on craters of Kepler and Copernicus.

Is tranquility the sea I can't reach
in my mind, sending rockets
that never land close to lunar craters?
Pastel-purple blossoms
are pressed into wet earth.
A persistent ambulance solo at Rusk
is accompanied by grackles, scents
of garlic from a nearby bistro
and of something serene I tried
to remember, yet it's gone
with the waft of a passerby's
Issey Miyake "L'Eau City Blossom."

We want to fly, to leave a flag,
a footprint at basalt bases
of all arrivals, but find
tranquility.

After Verdi's *Requiem*

When scars of fresh earth skinned over
more graves swathed in new-fallen snow,
I thought that many people promised to try
to live each day as the last, to sip coffee
with new morning blessedness of breath,
blend with a stream of people as though
we had no boundaries between our sorrows
and the muffled music we carry,
each singular melody similarly celestial
and differently distorted. Like the many,
acuity of resolution grew blunter in time.
I saw oblivious workweeks gathering speed,
the Ark of Family rowing in the Deluge.
I saw blossoms in a strobe light of short
time-lapses. Ice climbers belaying anchors
for followers. Skiers in blinding, faceted
sunshine of the vigorous life. I saw disabled
war veterans torturing their recent torturers,
hospices without anesthetics, my countrymen
in a line for humanitarian aid from the oligarchs
who set them against each other. I saw
posts on Facebook: laughing beach leapers
above "Life is Beautiful" scribbled in wet sand,
women in lotus asana — their thumbs and index
fingers held together, caption: "Let Love
be Your Frequency." I saw how frustrated
and easily annoyed are those who post them.

. . .

Whatever works, like my imaginary friend —
Pocket Woody Allen — used to say. I hope
some awful day, the One "who takes away
the sins of the world" will grant them rest
like in my recurring dream: I fall into a canyon,
but at the last moment something benevolent
that has always held me, lifts me in midair,
saves me from the earth.

El Pájaro
Gaia, "Marshland"

What is under your feet?
Friable clay several miles deep,
driftweed decayed, sanded
into sediment, ancient rock salt
pushed upward with oil seep.
What is above this soil?
Walking beams of pumpjacks,
migrant birds of marshland:
Whooping Cranes fly by day,
feed on the wing,
warblers peck in thickets,
flush in the dark
to the beckoning indigo.

What flock are you from
in the six-ward city?
I'd be a wordy nestling at Rice's campus
if I had flown in time — over the Iron Curtain —
to its Byzantine masonry.
El Pájaro ruffles up on the blue
security light. I am late,
jogging on Sunset Boulevard
to Moby's "Extreme Ways,"
with nothing to dash
except for my empathy
in broken English.

· · ·

Assimilation: *The Last of the Tribes*
looks back at the ancestral bayou,
Freedmen's town remains in a few
handmade pews in Antioch Church.
Will I survive the Texas scorcher
by my misplaced bullfinch song —
ruby drops spilled in the snow?

El Pájarito, mirenme a la vida vuelvo ya.
Polish me, foreign surf, like a pebble.
Gabled waves of rooflines are so high.
Freedom is warm
coffee at noon — in underwear,
working till ninety, like
Philip Johnson in his Glass House.
Someday I'll gaze at my forest
instead of wallpaper —
coastal mangroves,
Roseate Spoonbills, egrets.

Tree of Logos
Gunilla Klinberg, "Wheel of Everyday Life"

Plant the seed. Set the patterns,
Repeat until the wheel turns.
Watch bewitched like Ezekiel —
the cosmic tree burgeons, bears figs,
ashes, symbols, signs of Logos
unnoticed through foggy windshields.

The axis mundi is you, steering
in circles of everyday life, loss, logos —
a DNA helix, ascending
from the plan view of a sanded mandala,
a potter's clay spitted to the monotonous
hum of interstate roads that scared
the wits out of Wim Wenders:

Paris, Texas ... Texaco, Fiesta,
the moveable feast behind the ramp —
motley fonts in sideview mirrors
dance as a Sumerian calligraphy.
I squeal the hypnotic tune of Kashmir
to Led Zep on 94.5, while exiting to you
with a flask of SoCo tied to my stocking.

I think of my cousins in khaki
under the same sky in Iraq and Gaza,
and what is left of that Scarlet Tanager,
bare-foot teenager who strummed
"Holy the vast lamb of the middle class."
We diverge to absorb the scenery
from grade-separated flyovers
with different airwaves.

• • •

Aching Miracle

EZ tags. Coins. Om. Yum.
Whataburger — just like you like it.
How Sam Houston liked it.
Imperial Sugar for Tastykake.
A blue searchlight gropes for
its target group — Kmart shoppers
in Walmart distressed shorts.

Branded, marketed, discounted,
the oversized wheel, the abrasive
disc of the sand-filled mandala
keeps on turning:
                   Like us on Facebook.
A tender look at all related beings —
pulsating, vascular — becomes a habit.
An inflated rubber gorilla
waves from the Toyota dealership.

Houston Grandmaster
Dinh Q. Lê, "Crossing the Farther Shore"
— for my sensei, Grandmaster Van Binh

"Faster! Twist the stick in a figure eight —
it saved me, when scar-faced Somalis,
shouting in French, surrounded us.
I was a teen: no daddy to help,
no free *bánh mì*. When I was ten,
he stopped a French officer to return
our family valises. Coagulating
blood on my father's temple
is all I remember ...
Those who take the black belt test,
work on flying kick — respect
the school standards of Mr. Khan
who escaped from Viet Cong
after several years of torture."

My Master is eighty: I see
gouty feet under his pressed hakama
when he takes me down to the mat
with one acupoint push of his finger,
and the ingenious smile of an Olympic
boy from Saigon, who teaches me how
to make my opponent throw himself.
I'm bruised, my thin wrists ache.
At forty six I win sparring with
the sickly schoolgirl in me.

Mudman Running
Yusuke Asai, "Yamatane"

Mudman jogs repeating his jody,
Take my fears, make me a lighthead,
loving again all that's made from dust.
Mudman — lab dust with breath
blown into his nostrils — runs,
runs from wherever they know his story:
the more foreign, the better,
the quieter trail, the more healing.

Candid chalks and marls dart past.
Granites, dead-burned dolomites.
Shale-breakable, yet coarse, he is fast,
but sees all shades of clay under feet,
hears chirps of tiny creatures, notices
hidden life in puddles. He erases
pictures from his head: the former mudmen
pressed by caterpillar tracks into black earth,
his friend's arm he put into a rucksack,
so they would sew it back. Paramedic,
shoot that funky anesthetic — I'll sing.
Kitty-kitty, come with me, scraggy tramp —
I scream at night, but I'll feed ya.
Birdy-bird, don't shred that worm —
I've got seeds in my pocket.
They say, one day we'll be all washed away
like this bayou mud. Atoned
for the spilled blood. Running
at light-speed.

Kyoto Dolls

In my bedroom mirror are two black-haired Kyoto dolls:
pale, eyes closed, both wear brocade kimonos.
One doll is in indigo, the other in orange.
Missing the rope that once tied them together, they sleepwalk
toward each other, but get lost in strange places.
In a dream dark butterflies peer at the indigo doll
with magnified emerald eyes on their prophetic wings.
She hears the heavy breathing of a soldier,
working his way through a Guadalcanal rainforest —
his parched tongue reaches a drop on a glossy leaf,
a distant Scottish lullaby cools his fever ...
The microchip of inserted memories glitches.

The orange doll sees a bench at Bethesda Terrace —
Angel of the Frozen Waters sailing out of the fog, nude
branches in the whitewash morning of Central Park,
a piercing Eric Satie sadness played in a major key
by a jazz trio at Grand Central Station.
Greyhound buses depart to towns
grown around ghostly ships of chemical plants —
towns of disillusioned waitresses with deep V-necks
                                  and voices,
and blue-eyed workers with spent handsomeness
that you don't know whether to cry for, or leave alone
like that last cowboy on horseback struck trying to cross
Route 66. *Lonely Are the Brave.*

Donkeys prefer straw to gold, and it's nothing tragic.
Life unfolds like Handel's "Sarabande" from *Barry Lyndon*
through self-repeated intonation, the afternoon light
streaming sinful baroque tenderness to trailer interiors,
the unseasonable feeling of spring in January: that subtle
extra humidity, a ferment of causeless expectancies —
                                  Le feu follet,
metempsychosis that I assume about the wounded cats
that nuzzled into my life; tales of Kyoto dolls, one of whom —
with a glued-on head — is me? the soldier?

                                  • • •

Aching Miracle

For seven years you walked from the law office
through a cacophony of crossings, steam rising from subways
to the windy alien city. You looked for a silhouette
from the frosted window in the corner coffee shop on 42nd
until I came — dropped my rucksack next to you
and said, "It's time to go home." In the mirror
we finally meet on the shore. We are children.
I am in azure. You are in light orange.

Another April

               we can't reach Kyoto,
and I watch flickering footage of Kazuo Ohno
wringing his hands —
as a tottering female in a wide-brimmed hat
dances a surrender
to the flounder of death that swims within her.

He danced into his nineties:
lean, wrinkled like a dried flower,
but flexible, already more
a sensitive conduit for ghosts
than a body that danced his last Butoh
only with hands, then with eyes,
then breath, then as a phantom.

Another April
            we can't reach Hanami,
but I dance a blossom
with the urgency to unfold to full capacity,
I dance into the light
with the white makeup after Kazuo Ohno.

Tales of the Roman Moon

Snore, my dear, snore — otherwise
I'd be straining to your breath,
even if there is no reason to worry.
I'm with you in this room, this foreign
country, in the warm laser-thin web
of our breathes and uncertain itineraries.
Rome flashed through tunnels of our eyes,
the late night ride: superfluous Baroque
to electropop of a grooving driver,
piazzas where kisses are more cinematic
than at retail wastelands and all-the-same
bungalows in West Houston,
where I'm a foreigner too, but less so.

What is not foreign? Rooms
warmed with co-mingling breathes?
The full Moon sheds at us pale mercy
through a thin gap between curtains.
Every fifth of August in *Santa Maria Maggiore,*
white petals of dahlia fall from an opened section
in the gilded ceiling — *pioggia di fiori,*
ten minutes of summer snow for the Virgin Mary.
At nights, gore-scarlet petals
cover the ruins of Nero's *Domus Aurea* —
wild beasts roam in his dark gardens,
waiting for reckless guests and sleepwalkers.

Rome spills petals and oil.
There is nothing profane or holy,
nothing quenches thirst except wine —
temples of posh, pointless self-flagellation.

. . .

Aching Miracle

Bones of Capuchin friars — an object of art:
octagonal stars made of pelvic bones,
a coat of arms shaped with shoulder blades.
Chandeliers of vertebras — a few inches
above the head — don't teach me a lesson.
We leave catacombs, and I scold you
for something petty. And then I guiltily
pull the blanket over your bare shoulder,
listen to your breath, and imagine sunset
over our bungalow in Houston,
cannas I haven't watered for a week,
and my cats turning feral.

You Are Kind

— for my husband, Chris Juravich

It gets dark so early.
The black artery of a freeway clogs
with tail lights — scintillating
pomegranate seeds, dim ruby constellations.
Where are they all pushing toward?
Closer to Christmas I cling to you
as if I were sick, homeless, and you
were the only one who gave me a quiet
room with rare volumes, set the table.
I like to dine with you — not expected
to keep amusing talk or explain why
I did something wrong, how I used to explain
to others who I start forgetting. Though,
I recall the crisp, absent-eyed mornings
after Pinot-ruby nights — the floor to ceiling
window overlooking the misty, whitish Hudson,
my nude silhouette in spacious emptiness,
with a shiny green apple on the palm
for those who'd stylishly eat a serpent.

I become plain, warm-loving. Red
blurs my vision, Houston damp curls my hair.
"How are you doing?" "I don't dwell on it, ma'am" —
a tollbooth clerk giggles, his Levi's belted up
to his scrawny chest. "How are you doing?"
I greet a shamrock-tattooed shop assistant
rearranging canned cat food. "Living the dream."
Me too, and there is no irony, with
my home overseas bomb-shelled, friends shot
in the back by those who sent them to war,

. . .

Aching Miracle

and I have no one to exit from this highway
for a drink to the past grief. How could I
not live the dream, not thank the one
who is so kind to me? *"You are kind"* —
the last words of my taciturn father-in-law
to my husband's mom. It was in the ICU
where he asked me to put him on the ground
from his reclining bed, and found
sucking a tiny chunk of ice as a heavenly meal.
I knew so little about him: served in Korea,
gave blood for thirty years,
and never said anything cool.

Why do strong passions brandish
their verbose revolvers, but find refuge so quickly,
while Gogol's plain, provincial old-world landowners
silently sag when one of their mates die?
We don't dwell on it. Before Christmas
I skip the realtors' party and we drive to the mall —
not for shopping, but to walk hand in hand
under flickering snowflakes, sip hot chocolate
from one plastic cup to the same vintage tunes,
muffling the reality that season comforts hang
on a thin thread — *while* we are both alive.
Otherwise, the world would turn into a highway
clogged with strange cars, passing aloof in the dark
to unexplained darkness, pulsing with the brake lights
not nearly resembling Christmas decorations.

Six-winged Seraph ⁽³⁾
[black-and-white detail]
by Mikhail Vrubel

Aching Miracle

Glow

There is nine times more dark matter than stars,
floating in a symphony composers overhear.
For Stephen Hawking, the Universe
popped from an infinitesimally small
black hole, where time slowed to a standstill —
the No-Time to create the Universe: only
a hole to form a hill. Who dug the hole?
He is grateful for his random spark of life
in the fog of thinly spread clouds of matter.
Who's he grateful to? Should we
pass in silence what we cannot speak of,
shift inward to our own miniature galaxies —
the glimmering stellar fractals? Intellect,
skills for survival are collateral. A giant octopus
loses his blue-blooded arm, and it grows back.
Beluga whales have an IQ of 155 —
twice that of condemned men
in Huntsville state prison. The tree
of your blood vessels branches out
to the distance from Houston to Monterrey —
four hundred miles for oxygen to fuel
your thought which is, hopefully, kind.
What makes us human is not even eloquence,
but the sculpting of time in memories,
an invisible impulse developing its glow
on Kirlian photos — the luminous thread
between the reaching fingers of a couple in love.
This world is an *aching miracle*
whose touch no war can deaden —
sunshowers in the orchard of unsolved equations,
the symphony of dark
light years between the stars.

Elina Petrova
in her Aikido practice hakama

Poet's biography:

Until 2007, Elina Petrova lived in her hometown of Donetsk, Ukraine. Although her early interests leaned toward literature, philosophy, and the arts, her formal education followed a pragmatic track where she first received her bachelor and master's degrees in thermal engineering from the Donbas National Academy of Civil Engineering and Architecture and a second bachelor and master's degrees in production management from the Donetsk National Technical University. For several years following her graduations, Elina remained in her field through various assignments related to the design of utility plants and the promotion of industrial equipment. During those years, she also sharpened her literary skills, saw many of her poems and translations reprinted by far-reaching publications in Moscow, Kiev, and Donetsk, enjoyed the release of her first book-length edition of poetry, *White Square* (Белая площадь), and won the highest award at the First International Poetry Festival, Donetsk. Upon her emigration to the United States, she received certification in advanced paralegal studies from the University of Houston-Clear Lake. Elina now works in a Houston law firm, is an enthusiastic student of the martial arts, and enjoys advancing her poetic experience as a member of the Houston Poets in the Loop. Elina is a frequent featured reader in the Words & Art program at Rice University, has been published in many North American publications such as *Illya's Honey, FreeFall, Harbinger Asylum, Texas Poetry Calendar*(s), the annual anthologies of both the Houston and the Austin poetry festivals, was recently nominated for the Pushcart Prize in poetry, and was a finalist for the post of 2015 Houston Poet Laureate. Elina Petrova became a citizen of the United States of America in January 2014.